Liquidities

ALSO BY DAPHNE MARLATT

Ana Historic
At the River's Mouth: Writing Migrations
Between Brush Strokes (with Frances Hunter)
Ghost Works
The Given
The Gull *
Net Work: Selected Writing (edited by Fred Wah) *
Readings from the Labyrinth
Salvage
Steveston (with Robert Minden)
Taken
This Tremor Love Is *
Two Women in a Birth (with Betsy Warland)
Zócalo

* Available from Talonbooks

LIQUIDITIES

Vancouver Poems
Then and Now

DAPHNE MARLATT

Daphne Marlatt

Talonbooks

Talonbooks
P.O. Box 2076, Vancouver, British Columbia V6B 3S3
www.talonbooks.com

Typeset in Adobe Garamond
Printed and bound in Canada on 100% post-consumer recycled paper
Cover design by Typesmith

Cover image: Fred Herzog, *CPR Pier & Marine Building*, 1953
Courtesy of Fred Herzog and Equinox Gallery, Vancouver

First printing: 2013

The publisher gratefully acknowledges the financial support of the Canada Council for the Arts,
the Government of Canada through the Canada Book Fund, and the Province of British
Columbia through the British Columbia Arts Council and the Book Publishing Tax Credit for
our publishing activities.

The original edition of *Vancouver Poems* was published by Coach House Press in 1972 with cover
and illustrations by Michael Sowdon. Many of those poems have been modified and some have
been omitted for this collection.

Library and Archives Canada Cataloguing in Publication

Marlatt, Daphne, 1942–
        Liquidities : Vancouver poems then and now / Daphne Marlatt.

Poems from an earlier book: Vancouver Poems, have been rewritten and new poems added.
Also issued in electronic format.
ISBN 978-0-88922-761-3

        1. Vancouver (B.C.)—Poetry. I. Title.

PS8576.A74L56 2013   C811'.54   C2013-900097-6

The following recent poems, some in earlier versions,
have appeared in *A Verse Map of Vancouver*,
The Capilano Review, and *subTerrain*:

moonshine
after noon's
a lapsed
comes walking
animal sheen
raining buckets
this city: shrouded

| CONTENTS |

| THEN AND NOW |

This series of poems for Vancouver, in its address to the current, historic, and mythic aspects of the city, has been long in composing. *Vancouver Poems* first appeared from Coach House Press in 1972 as one of that publishing house's beautifully designed early books edited by Victor Coleman. It has been out of print for decades, yet seems to have lingered in a kind of afterlife through a few readers' memories. Talonbooks' request for a new edition initiated the resuscitation of most of the poems from the 1972 collection, which in turn led to my writing a new series in an attempt to come to grips with the massive changes that have continued to shape the city since the early seventies.

Vancouver Poems was a young woman's take on a young city as it surfaced to her gaze. Under this new title, *Liquidities: Vancouver Poems Then and Now*, the poems remain verbal snapshots, running associations that sound locales and their passers-through within a shifting context of remembered history, terrain, and sensory experience. Rereading the early poems with a current ear and eye of course led me to re-vision them, in some cases substantially so, in others less so. Picking up a pencil to alter some early orthographic habits like "&" and "thru" led to line lengthening, which sometimes affected their visual and verbal rhythm. Rereading the poems in 2012, I see I had already learned something back then from West Coast aboriginal art—the way forms emerge out of and appear within other forms. The syntax of these poems similarly forms and transforms, merging images in an ongoing flow. This rereading also led to a few changes in diction and, in some of those early poems, lengthier additions or deletions. Not all of the poems from the original edition are included here, only those I felt still had something to say about the city as it was when the 1960s were becoming those heady days of the 1970s.

As it was then: a town outgrowing its wooden houses, Edwardian temple banks and fog, a muggy harbour of shipping, a young city penetrated by water and beginning to register its multiracial, multicultural roots and branches, yet oblivious to First Nations presence both before its own beginning and still active within its boundaries. What might be the shape of such a city's *shite* or inhabiting presence, its ghostly energy for self-transformation? In the original *Vancouver Poems*, I had deleted the Japanese noh theatre word *shite* (or *sh'te*, closer to how it's sounded) from the opening poem, but here the word is restored to its active place. This is the underground import (in both senses), the unconscious question that drives the whole series of poems, then and now.

Vancouver's incessant deconstruction and reconstruction, its quick transformations both in (re)structured ground and in urban imagining, come further into play in the new series of poems, Liquidities (from liquid assets, cash, and increasingly from the incessant rain of global warming). The slower, more introspective rhythms of the city poems some forty years ago speed up as wordplay, faster image traffic, quicker jumps through milieux and temporal strata that intensify to verbal collisions in the new poems. Forest terrain faintly recalled in high-rise architecture. Wave trains of thought that oscillate between naming and transition. On edge, littoral, surfacing through the litter it leaves, the city's *genius loci* wavers in and out of focus through its tidal marks of corporate progress and enduring poverty. Through refacing and defacing. Through the changing faces of a metropolis driven by big name corporate backing, citizens shortchanged in the private rush to make profit at the expense of a faceless public. Yet these poems hear the quiet generosity of trees, the swirl of riptide rush, under all the changing *ings* and *isms*, some generative force like that which runs through words to make connection continue.

———

In that spirit of connection, warm gratitude to Karl Siegler, who so thoughtfully edited this book, and to Garry Thomas Morse who prompted and supported a new edition of *Vancouver Poems*, a project that initiated writing the new Liquidities series. Further gratitude to Susan Reid many years ago, to Daisy Sewid-Smith more recently, and to Trevor Boddy, for his observations of the city.

I am grateful to Fred Herzog and Equinox Gallery for permission to use his 1953 early-morning photograph of the CPR Pier and Marine Building, to Trevor Martin for permission to include three of his early 1970 and 1980 photographs of the city, and to the Historic Photographs Division of the Vancouver Public Library for use of earlier photographs by Philip Timms and Curt Lang.

A great many thanks to Greg Gibson for meticulous proofreading and book design, to Les Smith for cover design, and to Kevin Williams of Talonbooks.

Always deep thanks to Zasep Tulku Rinpoche, whose teachings keep enlarging my understanding, and to Bridget MacKenzie for encouraging persistence and sustaining my writing in so many ways.

Thanks to Albrecht Meyer for immediate tech support through both large and small emergencies.

I owe a debt of gratitude to many sources about the history of Vancouver, from newspaper clippings to current websites, but most importantly to James Skitt Matthews, the city's first archivist, particularly for the two volumes of his self-published *Early Vancouver*; also to Alan Morley, *Vancouver: From Milltown to Metropolis*; E. Pauline Johnson, *Legends of Vancouver*; Bruce Macdonald, *Vancouver: A Visual History*; Franz Boas, *The Social Organization and the Secret Societies of the Kwakiutl Indians*; Chuck Davis, for both *The Vancouver Book* and his website on Vancouver history.

And great appreciation to Colin Browne, Meredith Quartermain, George Stanley, Roy Miki, Fred Wah, Sharon Thesen, Maxine Gadd, George Bowering, and the late Robin Blaser, writing companions whose poems about here live with me.

| VANCOUVER POEMS |

Car je est un autre.

ARTHUR RIMBAUD

Wet fur wavers

              up a long eye-line Sunday sprays
interior city ground. Aqueous cut of the sea's
a bottomless lagoon. Logs lash on. The grey
stretch of sand I walk, footsteps sucked. jumped.

Changes air now wet as the sea, the *sh'te*

comes walking up through humor in the way of
vision, salt. Cedar all over. Cedar for headdress.
Beaver or bear, what is there to the touch of,
you said. Come well back into view.

                      Trappings, change,
what runs in the middle, gestures, wired for
vision. Spiral back through city even underground

(the esplanade traffics in waves to the point
that all of your faces echo, through one I. white.

Small figures as blue and white when shadows come,
down alleyways of sight, peri winkle, *vinca*, small
single flower

             by the sea (Salt does. Asphalt
cuts through time, your eye, my tongue, down where a
culvert mouths on the beach the city's underground:
you come through walking, corpses, bits of metal,
bird cry.

Lagoon,

            down a cut on the city side, apartments
stacked uphill, through shadow and hulls and ribs we walk.
You've come home.   On either side dark nets remember
how a wind fishing for that extent both left and right
ruffles your hair. Here. The city drinks what it collects.
Water or ducks, a nesting place. A neck of land.

Whose profile somehow looks more narrow in the street.
Our eyes reflect … kites, banners, a populous sky.
What you or others brought, come back to
                                        Lie when we
outwalk our dragons, thus, their future tails: catch on
fire.

You confirm that we sail to the east at nine, shore wise
having no place, antique, a houseboard. Wind ships our
ship, stands, having completed its turn to, gather to
exit, under the bridge …

            Wait! I can't get my hand out of green
pockets green,   dissected,   frogs. The edges of their
vision littoral. We skirt red.   I'm half in, wanting to
pull up reeds to plant.

            Your coin proves nothing, no
bottom, don't. Go (in shoes sucked under). Water
scuttles old men on benches under conifers. Listen:
their edges always murmuring, Marshes, Your
forced march.

Could we afford your leaving? A salmon run? On the
corner there, half indecisive, tarnish of atrophied
fish in raffia swung: a house sign, a place to
enter.

            Where I'd make tea, your lips on the future,
caught, so you could read me.

Past ten,

          a night so luminous kohl
glistened when she snatched the flower, in an
eyeblink.   We were still, walking.   Light pours
blatant from Coke sign to our feet. We step through
(hands) the pavement slides under, cerements,
earth slides, only the cracks hold.   At points
across the city Chinese grocers throw wide palms
of light,   bamboo slats ring down on, Begonias
(cash registers blank zero and zero) crash in their
tinfoil

          No one came running, if eyes saw (she
expects?)   I expect sea light in yours I'd seen
almost a year ago.   My prospect changes ...
digging for salt water taffy, or the tin flare
windows strike.   Pipe in pocket.   Nothing.

                              ... cups her chin.
Who's kind of a flower, who's kind to, is that,
you?   If you stole, what kind of a flower would you
... verbena, violet, vervain ... seep in the blood.
A slow crystallization might hold him who
tromps between. Six feet down the grass in cracks
grows, absurd, most impossibly green.   He has
eyes for. What? What she thinks is the sense of
his pockets torn with want. Involved with windows,
or eyes. She's throwing tulips at faces, tipping
her heart out to them.

                    I open the car door, they
climb in.   Salt grins in my lips I'm on the other
side of, hair, here, in the wreck we ride down to ...
red light. Go, go, she says, go. No one pays for
the flower.

'Old bird', he

        turned up thin this time, bones
held together by yellow and translucent parch /
meant rags and bags and papers. His torn collar,
scarf at so craggy and knotted a neck declared
itself to be holding the trachea, thin rind of
muscle. When he opened glass to admit me a
skeleton stood in the broom cupboard where the
toilet was. I sat. Clotted broom bristles
hugged the wall. All around, coughs, creepings
of old men trickle in under the door.

At night I hear him hack up blood, scrape it up
with his tongue (head against mine on the other
side of cardboard). Parrots in wallpaper mimic
the sound.

        Upstairs, went to hand him the
cheque, his room a shell sucked dry and filled
with granular bird tongue. He without his
jacket (rheumy eyed), let loose the scarf,
sagged into abandonment.

        Sunday you were young
still, there. We sat, surrounded by glass panes that
fell out one by one from the windows. Drank our
coffee, ate boiled eggs, solemnly. And all the bells
of all-day churches round about were throwing up
their clappers.

Femina

                 you who
                          fail,
                                  subtly seeking, with your face
angled downward to the floor, to cups, to broom
slivers in the cracks, to sea below,   to hands
and feet of people walking in proximity to you.
Who wait, up in your room that sideways to the
street holds certain figures in a gloom.

When the whiteness of light casts its sheen over
your face, you sit reading. Your eyes seem closed
in their downward looking, in the electric   .
enumeration of eyes of strangers reading you.
And bedposts, glutted with the heads of fishing
corks, which you, as yet, will still hold on to.

All
       evening
                 air slowly darkened round the windows
you were caught in, rings on a glass jar. Coherent
images of light fist into themselves after the bulb
has gone, just, out ... (It's then the rock cod
drift up through blankets of the sea to reach you ...

They flung the door open onto the city. You saw
her framed: her long green laver skirt, ankle-tied,
heels poised on your fire escape. The precision of
those heels. Paused, in third position, knees bent,
one fishy sleeve out, to the door ...

                                  O the fabulous
laugh of the sea trapped in a jar (o the tearing of
water
          where you are

The bones of your face are pinned with syllables,
sea wrack, a drift of other rhymes.

Morning

        makes that light up billboard face a time we
near you, clear the air we stuttered in, mid, last
night's news ...

        Be side, by side, Beside the
water's edge we come up to, ignore bridge-wise, say,
the siding of houses dark, or dank with what sea
does. There is that smell the air will never get rid of.
Riddled. Or crushed by ground come up. Gravel.

We could believe in grass growing through cement in
parking lots they've turned their yards into. This bill
board fronts a house, or sides it, ferry sidling above an
abyss the bridge ... Black Ball, You, ferried into high
seas of the mind.

        This time skin has touched
thin air, raising rumour. Bones razed this morning,
ear honed in the sharp gaze of a gull, bridge-poised,
momen/tarily, the rail he
perches on

        for purchase. Specific to your head the waves
loomed above, late, in street light's desolate glare it's
pitch and drop, Where you were, two of you, on the billboard
ledge, swinging your legs. *What* ...? the cop who stopped. Only
getting some air, sir ...

        It is not instant, these houses blind to
the bay. It does not recognize a sign, this news (whose?)
rammed to the wall night has seeped into. It's constant,
rain, raising your collar, raising

    grey linoleum
    burst tomato, mildew sill,
    roach stain in the wood rotting,
    no-name

What a rock thrown in, hit by
design, by what casual will to break in / out /
through …

Black Ball's *Chinook II* on
schedule, churns through troughs and peaks. It does not
fail. is not found, wanting. You want, you are found
cut to the quick. Under grassgreen light a mercury vapour
lamp pours out, For hope, halloo, hallucinatory,

shatters love sometime.

Light, gets

        the way sun fills a, silhouettes,
pavilion (dirty), floss of worn. sandstone.
bodies warm. Sudden increase wind off water
rakes. A stare. Cold hard measure there.

On wash house wall is writ: Sun / God for a day.

Sea bathing made this,
                Show ground of knit
wool costume, black, brolly flounce. Later
lavender promenade, hipswivel, thinly
clothed, a look ...

longest days of the year this weekend mean, late
from the Sylvia's beer, sun divine, chain, some boats,
no guard
        (Joe in bronze ...

                bandstand a grand
stand watch, circuitous. full path going down of
sun, moons coming on. low glow. popcorn stands,
their friends, dogs, small knot a cigarette makes,
shared joint, incense in the

                act of living this
continuing thread, drawn to water's edge
where

        suit/ably appointed, self begotten, Swimmers'
Guard he lived, a natural. No quit-job, called (Seraphim
of Barbados) to sun's loom, intersection of
                low light and
      water
        (winging it? No

seasonal fly of want, stayed as the popcorn sellers do,
warming hands (moths) to, late light's hot butter drawn
this winter long.

Robsonstrasse

        Käsekuchen under glass,
baby on one hip outside a bakery, stopped, by
exclamations in the traffic patterns of the past.
4711 and salami, Frenghe's eggs, print whiff of
European news   hausfraus in their rush barely
notice
     Chinese girl unhurried

                 waters down her pots
their pricey shoes

      Who

         knows these streets
like the Greek? waiting on park bench in black, dusty,
all his pockets worn with want,   Kids in wading don't
understand, He wants to be, "oh waiter" white-
towelled in the top-hat Aristocrat, so Ritzy? / No,
a *diner* means ... threadbare count. For washing
dishes, he said, I come?

       Not that his old-world civility's
unpriced. The market changes image-wise. Can he
make her who would, back to his room's geranium some
other left, deny

        The fury of his look it circles her,
gulls,   wading pool,   girls—   What is a misprized tool?
mistaken want?

      Simply, momentarily free, cotton
skirts about them they fly the building (shadow) for the
small trees, wind, the traffic brings, lights. They
want to swim,

     (aren't you hot in your black suit, Dimitri?)

O strasse. hanging roasts, piazza. and the day's dust.

Slimey,

                         mackerel sea-sky (eyes down). Limed
public library steps, the gulls. Mean what they
cry. Time, time.   How many stoop to a dead fish?
How would you like a tail in the eye, scales, a
little bit rheumy but other/wise …   Off the point
they go fishing.   Under latches of the bridge,
rusty, rattling their rods.   Tide.   Swirls down
deep there. Noon reigns in the street, a White Lunch.

Blue hubbard figures hump, endless round. The Cup's
too big to get into. Would it hold anything but rain?
Steams on a hot day, the park lunches.

Hold my hand in this cracked vinyl booth where
bread wilts.   I love you but don't, fling your rain-
coat over my head.   It smells, wet. Hair hangs into
my cup.   Love rains.   You will go far somewhere.
Where? matter inserts relation.

Peels, heels, float like hulls of hands under the
wharf. Rats dockside.   Carrying orchids up, and the
port, and the starred-on-board lights.

Milk run Amalia ends up on library steps, a cigarette,
some soup.   A wet day steams up the insides of
their eyes.   I want to know how gulls keep flying.

"It's rained

                    the last 10 days!" They say IT meaning
what?

          Credence for wings still cloud, mountain back, to
back,   far as an eye etc only high up, frayed, inhuman
rush of, Rage? Knows no such
                              element we live in, dull,
sense of outrage at the mercy of.   Razorback woman
down a cliff edge. Hurt the sea wind curls.   No good
food can stomach: Sea a
                         seam of shoes (canvas curling,
gills or, sea anemone)

                                   Air everywhere.
Liquid weight clung, to aery lungs not destined for,
cough,   that crevice of rock,   foothold,   fingers do,
in their cold claw-like.   Emma, permanently bent.

Say her frizz of hair eyes stare from (anger, without wings),
Pocket those stubs with some tobacco (few) and thaw,
vulture of The Bay young mothers avoid.

                                   For hours or days.
Place to reach out from. To what?   Rain does it, still small
voice (peewit) internal rooms.   This drip/drip persists.
Making up, light rags of this or that, a continuity
badly joined

          Toward what end?

                         The run-through all there is a
tide, none better, felt now as   . High   . combats crack in a
wall of downtown litany mass't nicotine speed etc toward

On grass down "Victory" square the tenuous arrangement
pigeons have,

          Or rain keeps falling white / lightens or

"Our city is ashes"

                     in the curve of all that water, False
Creek, Burrard Inlet, detonating bombs on cleared lots, gun
powderers out for   Timberrr! Wood shacks, two-by-fours,
plank sidewalks incendiary, a, crematorium, in

                                   which
there was a man, driving horse and wagon, caught on
Carrall Street between Water and Cordova … two iron tires
and some ashes was all that was left …

                           of our city, our
city is, *swept clean to the bare black earth*, a mess of
charred stumps, molten bell smoke-enveloped, human
remains,

    That labour too, consumed.   A watch, identified one
of *twenty-one parcels of charred fragments—not bodies—*
each with a pinned note telling where it was found.

Where, from memory trails cleared space, amid the embers,
naming such and such hotel, establishment, whose ice house,
whose front parlour … said he had their pay stuffed in his
pockets, To be safe,

                     There was a current of cool air close
to the water we were standing in, between the heat and smoke
and the surface of the water; we breathed it, and it saved us.

                                     It
is not separate, what we are standing in.   Cannot be separated off
the skin or internal, marrow, bronchiole. *They had been blowing*
stumps on the CPR Hill, they had been razing bush, they had cleared
for the railroad, knocking trees down wholesale. *The whole of the hill*
above Victory Square had been afire for weeks … Cannot be separate
from what we breathe. This too-easy 'victory'

                      Our city is ashes   three thousand
people homeless Can you send us any government aid?

                                                        Acrid
in the nose, as federal government's delay.

                                        Our citizens are
in extreme want   Will your Gov't please do something for us?

Are in, our citizens, in tents by the sea, in lean-tos, in
hunger, in a sea of smoke
                              While, miraculous,
was it? an *Act of God* some said,   Fire turned back at
the mill, this pre-town's raison d'être spared, Wind
freshening, changed direction some say, Some who saw
the freshets still down mountain rain, down mountain
water shed the moment clearing

                              Smoke-drift, speck
in the eye, later citizen blur on the way to

                                   make a bundle

Wood waste by beehive burner, sawdust to ash, consigning
fish to …

                    In which the ex / outside / extinct
(twenty-one parcels of charred flesh) enter as present
 residue we

                    Cannot, rid our selves of

"Spectacular"

        CPR's new pier, gangway descent, water lap at
building's back, open harbour. Turret front, its portico wide
sweep of waiting room, Custom's sticky city entry: Pier D
long-timbered wharf that thousands walk

                  in time, Seabirds
trawling wind.
            Incessant, shipping

    several transcontinental trains daily
    white *Empresses* from the Orient calling

passenger disembarkation, for, he remarked with pride,
the coming metropolis.   High-buttoned boots a stamp of
civility. Lions chasmic yawning. Royalty on a cowcatcher
view the Rockies. O Empire's furthest outpost cradled
by inland sea the ships go down to. And they crowd
around   as so many shadows view the new arrivals

Gateway to ... capitalize (on) a labour pool, their East our
western sun, sets a time of *terrific coolie movements ... The
Chinese were going through Canada in transit and were
heavily guarded* THIS WAY (only)

                  Unseen from the first
reverse:
        'Back home' THAT way: lace, pianos, lamps, all
tinkly equipage,   by royal steamer

                  (*Celestials* pig-tail
tied, shipped to Victoria, no siree, no *Chinee* loggers in the
Brighouse claim)

        "At-home" refugees from rain
chatter of opera house   blue willow ware   *The Geisha*
that "infernal houseboy"   standing near

tea and silk

first thing off the ship and onto the train east ... silk train ...
heavily insured

         against time or accident or loss (whose?

a virtual holocaust,

         unreal they said of *Flames ... traveling*
underneath the dock ... mock civility rules o citizen ... *at a*
terrific pace, Fireman Bird had *difficulty getting down the*
Granville Street hill ...

         so thick   was it

with viewers,   inferno-drawn.

Free . free the

                 dead dreaming, mercenary, of some
token. of their worth. Holes. One wet loafer
equals two, three, beer,   herself bargained for

                             Gift-giving
a pride once, a name, lived up to. Unhoused now,

slave to hotel parlours and their musty carpet
corridors, their puke tile floor green painted, white
man's sickness for

Her. Survival takes. Vision, skill, canoe race harbour's
open (choked) light. Eyes' quick glint, not for money,
but laughter, pride … Beyond the tin roof steeple rise,
tracks, bush traversed by
                       inroads money makes.

Take the Tomahawk displays its relic clubs, dust-grain
carvings acquired and oohed at over hotcakes, pass-the-
maple, beach-blonde fries …

With salmon bury bear and other equals: woods, sea,
sky.   Mountain bears its own remains, dismembered
hand, fuselage.   A marshgrass mist the slipways waver
through. They wait, who never depart …

                       No end in sight,
but the weekend carload of groceries and kids, illegal
beer.   For what? gold crucifix?

Time does not redeem the city, bringing it all up, how,
Pacific Centre, under the pavement of parking lot

foundation of old hotel, and then some dirt (lumber, coal)
some trail to clamshells …

For what part: my city

                                monotonous under cloud bank hums,
throttle unseen, barge accidents, the fog.   Merged with its
rocky margin, rain, tree arms (dripping dark) a dilute
sun records ... scuttle of crabs in the soaked bark. Sudden
jerk, steamy, tug snap, (april oolichan run salvation),
no sound towing's quite complete without ...

    (hands, all, downed in water swell)

Not stumps of cabbage field-wise rot, in an echo of axes,
Jerry's spar, the swell. Men on springboards balance pre-
carious, halfway up a trunk, hack (largest floating limb in
the world ...) crash to the undergrowth

    (snug plaid jacket, rainhat, remnant of a foot)

Even pubs this evening, closed, levy their tribute for a
Salvator none care to know.   Cross in the harbour dark.
Signals RR hotel, the Main (skid) roads annex.   Spittle of
stairway yields its boards' last crack, last, gulp ...

                              What travels west?
besides suicide, a stake in the string the junk shops pawn?

This city: shrouded (shreds) of original stands, darkened by
absence of (at the foot of Columbia Tea Swamp joined the
water's edge), its will o' the wisp, is Bukwis, old
                                        ghost

figure of woods.

To navigate

        grey-green fathoms, un/fathomed
intent, a word to be applied only eye-desire,
hands, hips, lift, body parts in sync, incline (rise)
to join ... what am I then, air? (tug, that makes a
bridge rise, by which, bewitched, I feel your thrust,
my lift, want

        not sky, that inch by inch
straining upward intent ...

        Bridge circuit snapped, red
light flashing,   heads into autonomous
alien ...
      sky / gap / electrical ab
             sense air is,

how it parts, struck by down-descending
weight to hold   (just for a

        Second

           Narrows, as it was

once, coming down. Tide swirls under long gone
bridge lumbering flat now, trains roll on

low bascule (buttocks), suck of tide requiring greater
clearance for this inlet's "bridge of sighs" two freighters
hit, then *Pacific Gatherer* knocks out its span. Erect
deck, jackknifes to sky

        gap, a break

in the crossing tide swirl to green, still green North Shore
rail lines and traffic propose, despite Depression, vertical
lift span that will (will it?) clear shipping. Red light flashing
NO   farther ...   watch that span shudder into sky above
steep bore wave, the tide

        that swallows men.

Third try crossing, new high-level cantilever reach out to
… (air) …

                         jumble of twisted truss span steel
workers flung from / to, murky tide divers lift bodies from.

Now at night, near Chay-chul-wuk, *near or narrow*, lost
ironworkers ghost on through   intent   on

the join)

Go on

       go on along Main, along the way light lingers in the
goldfish bowls junk shops are made of, junk, a ship, to
sail away on, to opulent shores a commode, old needles,
her gathering flesh knows nothing of.

                       She choked on the
contents of her stomach. Mostly alcohol.

                      Or sitting alone
along the curb of public buildings, old Carnegie Library
closed down. Men. Pigeons. Shit all over the stone.
Thighs crossed, disowning their feet down steps where
they go, who can't wait to make it / to score / to go on

                        Agile
wits necessary as the need. Chew that off, the cash,
no teeth to flash.

                    She dyed her hair
flaming red, her flesh grew inches on her as time did in the
pubhouse chair. Shit, man, just gimme a bed, I don't care.

Who writes the inter-office memos? Who built Dominion
Trust? Who reached the top of the Sun?

                    Pigeons dreaming,
mordant lustre to their plumage. Greens, purple. Bruise.
Fittest for what milieu?

                    She missed the chair,
scrambling over it to reach her, fell, heavily on a wrist
(hurt? ... get away!)   and came up laughing, If cocaine
does that, I oughta try a beer maybe ...
                    seven hours after
release, was found dead.

Who eats in this pond?   At arm's length,
mostly bone.   Outside, cars eat at the city's lungs, mills
chew away at the source,

                              SOMEBODY's banquet
of flesh goes on.

Trails

      frayed paths leading, leaving … one-way sits,
stoney, picks at, loose end of her, at loose ends, waiting.

      Beer. In beer she sits, loud, in laughter,
Stanley or New Fountain nights of rain. Fog warning
loud and long. Low swish of cab, slow (in the sharp
scythe, of cop headlights …)

                    Used to see her, beach
side of Water, one block down. Seep into her sitting,
wet, in rough wool socks. Rim the coaster edge, sodden,
ground by pebbles, fingers, all hands leave

                nevah, nevah a trace …

No more shattered by than one is seeing trees, whistled at the
heart of her, his words will cut

      You SPENT it! Bitch!

                Entrepreneur, white,
with native "leman" come to beach his Union Jack and
joviality, a simple first (cash) inroad to Maple Tree's
black hat talk of *what this town needs*, Carrall 'n Water'ng
hole, to drain a cup, to drown their whiskers in, and meet
her Indian eyes …

      Hastily, someone's idea: *Maple Tree Square
would rival the public spaces of the world* where

Drunks shuffle in shut-down doorways, tired christmas
lights, all year beer parlour fights, thin-chested
bird whistle, their dyed hair and tongues. The bond
still ("head" offered, a toke) or known by the
streets they keep, ghetto or someone, hey, Maggie,
knows you …

Entrances

        speak doors that swing under
men's, women's (*and escorts*, escorted by an era
gone a little later than the sawdust, smashed glass
brawls, still, the angry sweep of hand or
beer-clumsy (weighted, rolling to the floor

    (root's daughter's o
                the waiter, watch where
you're going, threatens (snarl) big beer belly's
MUSCLE
      means, to the door bounced exit onto
                    (desolate
light, no,   POWER

        back there where friends, where
the world sits on curved chairs by little tables stacked
with glasses, empty, full, empty, waiter, eight more
(weighted) take one for yourself, change
wet on the

      Changes,   change is. floor caves under
BaxbakuālanuXsīwē's body "covered all over with
mouths," drops, to the pit, his red cedar bark falls,
into the hands of hāmats'a

         a drumming and a singing
pulse, rock charged air smokes (the red smoke of
his house? smokes Mountains, *at the Mouth of*
river-running sea

       Whose heart heavy with ferocious lips,
to see, legs, hips, tits, to want? the taste of flesh,
or whose small hair.

              With a violent gesture wipes out the
bar, the primitive order of barkeep, bouncer, copcar, court
or,
   construction
                       (*use the men's entrance*) is the construction
we put upon it, his glass, his chair someone takes or someone's
eyeing up his girl. *Men's, women's.* the separate washroom
doors they vanish into. The private law. He said I put the
finger on him, picked up outside, fingered, it is all alien,
property, Is what belongs to another, Her tight dress no
trespassing but still, come in—
                      We live by (at the mouth of)
the world, and the ritual. Draw strength Is not Secret
a woman gives (in taking, Q'ōminōqa) rich within the
locked-up street. Whose heart beats here, taking it
all in,

     Nānwaqawē: Who are you?
     She: Your daughter (didn't you know? Initiator.

Who is rooted to the floor with a root so deep he cannot
shovel it. Singing:

The hāmats'a mask of the forehead, the hāmats'a
mask of the whole world, the prettymask ...

       and

The red cedar bark of the whole world is making you
voracious

       ...

             O little man, o little man with dull eyes,
with three full glasses at closing time, I take you in.

Terminal

       rewind, of a line (trolley tracks limp back toward).
Open its doors to the crumbling of transfer. thin.   One or
two,   however late, descend,   rescind, habitual glare light
for whatever reason
                   straight, in the face of harbour's
rank wild smell.

Pilings eaten away at the foot, a stutter of docks, jetties,
jutting where the ferry used to run, broaching the swell,
low down (gasoline pools, peel, whatever refuse
refused its meta/
            morphosis.

Inside glass, coffee bar steam. Outside cars wet, crew in
slickers on deck, rain deafened, wind, fading into wave ...

              At the foot of a steep
descent is Vinick's used furniture (mirrors, chairs), Oreck's
five and ten, Eskin's unworn fabric smell.

The body of the esplanade suffers (who walks?) Emptiness.
Of dry dock, warehouse. Who, with his eyeball to plate glass,
a dummy's night waxen skin, under the green light with
nowhere to go, thinks, in a ghostly clatter of bowling pins,
to make time (whether in fact or no), says so ...

                       Taxi!
Where the reservation, babysitters, sleeping dogs don't lie.
Down, where the end of the town's

         a street without a car
         a car without a man
         a man without a name,

                 Night, ah.

The body of the esplanade sunsets, colours of gas. Works
tremendous visionary marbles crowned HOTEL (o *abal* on)
whose registers see pseudonyms and dreamers, drunks,   reign,
their collarbones in doorways. Weathering.

Park, ground:

                     Vancouver dreaming early, cold-bound.
Coal Harbour wraiths, three of them, knew early foliage
in excess steaming. Now from bridge space, the
tracks, the lumber stacks all traced, white. Have
winters gotten colder?

                         Know this only old
CNR station by the Ivanhoe, its concourse echoey glass
solder holds, grease shafts stamping (cold) muscle bound.
Steam, even diesels do. Track once wet ground (Creek
waters) since reclaimed

                        re? railways' claim to
ground this city rails built

                     Roads in rainforest

dark through park woods (before the storm of '62
cleared it), ribbon sky lowers, snow. Chasm coming
on, First Narrows flanked by concrete lions, Cable-
hung, the bridge, Soars. Rear lights flaring red to
white, to, mountain ...

                   Snowed-in wooden house, no, they
don't switch on the lights, sit watching night creep
up on them. Dusk smell, Wet cedar reach, encroach
... cedared everything, put mildly away. In hope
dispose of fungi, mold, damp clothes. A mean
resistance to the cold survival makes, the line
                               drawn

where coal brought them first to settle Brickmaker's
Claim, *from Burrard Street* (Burrud, she said) *to Stanley
Park, and from the inlet to English Bay.* the English
drawn to bricks, pots, stability, mark, of mother
country to be. Established here, no time lost.

Wood everywhere in excess felled like *bowling pins* ...
little coal, no clay.

Not til later heard: alien something in stone, *only Indian eyes could discern*, its inhospitable presence fixed in place by old-growth Chinook trees,

a blowdown.

Old wood

        shoes sink in. mulch. toes curl away from,
crumbles in the hand some (late) stump heart. Only
casing what was, is, riddled with weather, riddle of
achieved height now

                            desuetude or, crumbs left
pieces dangling (shreds) the wood ticks, worms
eat through

        to
                air, acrid and earthen. Water
brackish, fern the dead wood's only

                    green

                            moment,

Monument, on the edge, Pioneer Mill then Moodyville,
and from Hastings Mill, small fires curling up, saw
whine at water's edge the. chips. fly where they
will. But not, not *Moody's men went dry and
worked sober.* From each, inlet adrift with it,
Smoke ...
           a sea   Bear comes down through, mountain
ravine, eyes watering, small eyes red, windows set,
the sun, catches early.

                  Be changed, grow fur (logs at sea do),
be Bear Mother screwed by a bear's, by a giant

                  (will, make Moodyville, the dryest
                  settlement the inlet's, financial
                  success

                        who died at sea).

What we called "fort," its bark exterior still stands,
jagged and high enough to crouch in, fingering
what scrapes under nail, palmlines silted with it,
listening, for what?

Cedar wood carved and painted, will stand tall mid
dark the branches weave now, place abandoned as a
burned-out house

        To represent, flaunt (haunt) the
would-be EVENT, whistling in the deep wood.

West Coast oh,

        ecco, echo cistern, leaching the heart of
mountains water reigns. their flanks watershed outspread.
Innumerable roots, fine, horsetail and bryophyte. Up,
all the way up, tallest of douglas fir in some places
almost
        "kings"
          in-
            spire their grey day, this,
uncountable succession of half-knowing *here.*

(Vancouver: charts and instruments take over, or, 1890,
Robert M. Fripp, *Our object on this trip was to*
spy out the land

       / Discern

        branch limit fingertip its scope oh,
within reach what clusters, what is drawn, all, inter-
known   osmosis and the transformations of

        In this strange, weird lost sort of place
Rip Van Winkle might have played bowls with Hudson and
his ghostly crew ...

       Civil, eave drippings now, trough down
cement channel out, to sea

       (*First water crossed the Narrows Monday*
night at 11:10 March 26, 1889, *a valve was turned ...*)

       In the mouth of, culvert,
sewer, cistern,   as from underground uprisen Orphée,
water's welling

       Drawn, ultimately, from *Kiapilanogh*,
downstream roots, myriad dragonflies and minute creatures
make, diaphanae, mineral silt, what wood ticks engage in,
not parasitic, nourish, ruby crested etc breathing (wings)
air itself wet, steeps

Arising and flowing under cork at

HEART:

water we drink.

Spring's

                         new leaf chestnut fuzz red wings and
tires down King Edward curve a slick of wet, some muck—
time's mostly—almost green, so new even pavement
shines. Prim
                eaves (rainhat over old cheeks) late sixties
thin arm barrier holding traffic up, compact of squirrel
fur and camphor dust, step out

                              Rain steep. telephone
pole creosote. limbs of apple. saturate with the wet they
absorb ...

Dog-headed stick's his voice, dreary (tore down the hatter's
over on Granville. mad for dove silk, pins, his mourning
coat—*our ladies always helped to the door*—

                             the cemetery's

municipal water sieve a ghost, aghast, kids conscript sip,
houses bordering asked: how does your water taste? These
few days of rain make. Dandelion history

           or tripe, dressed and white. Bacon makes
eating comfortable. Whose shoe, on the right foot can she
bend (an ear) the Scot in stained apron knows, kipper in
string, whatever, other habits pose
                     a tea, a drowning

sorrow tolled in the steamed-up café. Swallow mornings'
not-yet trace, eave nests.

               Cabbage and apples out of delta
truck farm, Model T, weighed and, Wrapt she hovers
watches him balance weights, calculate, small silver dimes.
accumulated raindrops' shine.

No public eye, thus, takes what it can (water the city's
element) but breathes it, bleeds it, multiplies ...

Under

      the steady drip of conifers at night, Slow, glow worm,
Rains drive home. Eats earth while night covers something
shines, *lampein.* no more than possibility, lampyridae.

Winged? hardly. Tell, they're fishing for you under
cover of the earth, small one caught. Whose soft
abdomen shines, all desire there. eyes closed,
breathing in   Want— what?

Or even know you do   til bread, milk, lure is in
your mouth, open, crying.

To dwell with conifers. Eaves drip, echo cedar's arm
shedding water down   Spray scales waxy (cover
you lost.

Into a band of light the open window shines. No house can
stand for long under incessant rain. Though cedar grows
arms out, welcoming. This new light in water means

carboniferous imprint of old fern, echinoidea, solaster,
we step back in space before the drift and diamond light
fail—to call

Worm, small worm host of light.
Borrow a shell.

| SOME OPEN DOORS |

*They had arrived at the water's edge with
their violins and pianos, some books,
some pictures, ideas, undoubted aspirations,
opinions—or nothing whatever.*

ETHEL WILSON

innuendo

White Lunch anyone—not marble
nor the starch of keep-out aprons faded now it's looser
anecdote a little blue all manner drawn to warm from
grey outside while fiction strands yellow and orange
lantern holes in the dark light slices from

　　　　　—cut me a piece of that nice pie,
　　　　　　　　　　　　　　　　　will you?

　　　　　　　　　　　　　　　　　　　　catch her

eye from solitary booth striped neon cup a photo op of

comic cut-outs hurried trot with tray round saucer's
endless one-time spinster jaunty newsboy gaffer

pale eyes from face long in bone he shifts one withered
leg to leave a coin

　　　　　—you goin' now?

mugs setting out in rain arranges cap

　　　　　—know where I went last night?

　　　　　　　　　　　　　　　　　　I distinct
went / want for no place to go against the anonym her face
displays no interest

　　　　　—you know where!

his laugh her shrug the time it takes *intime* fake brass
reflects used shine of coffee mug she lifts to wipe
his place clean

moonshine

start!   for the tracks   let's go let's start   February morning dark
not dark but full   end of the alley   end of a night full moon rides
telephone poles bar the sky   moon's face a shine we take to

go! let's go he says eager to start for the tracks for the train for that
idea south   moon stays *allons!* night-alley intent   half-pulled from
sleep to wipe the windshield   lunar light makes moist

clearing glass to stare   all dewy one   dew-dropping down-
turning through wires and poles that scaffold west   a buzz still
spawning old woes old   moon in her shoes   shed   spilled
scattered abroad

                        the way they came   building where water was
on the edge of the tracks a litter of shacks little of what began a bright
idea: *west* they came   drawn by the rails by work by song   a trade
on rhythm and wit

                        east of us the rooflines sharpen now

let's start! he cries   my eager child   in the wane of the year's moonshine
one ray of, on a sleeping woman Musaeos her son moon mad or moon
inspired   his storehouse of stories bright in the dark   a mothering
eye inside that broods   brooms   beams down passageways

our future almost light on the other side   not morning yet

some of them got off the train and just walked in like they'd been
here before *at six or seven o'clock in the morning you'd hear …
jukeboxes going, somebody hammering the piano, playing … guitar*
click of the dice   big talk   someone's neighbourly cask uncorked

in the crack between two dawns   cop knock

let's go he says as if unsaid he longs to leave behind for the new
this low-lying ground between two waters   thick with story

lucent the rails not CN now but elsewhere leading south of here
not dark but full where memory talks up laneways *wide enough
for horsedrawn carts   and the horse ran away   alee*   their words
a gallery we drive along   and *en passant*
know where we are in light of their stories.

reading it

see what the cards what the roads say? no road to a place
where there is no trouble

                          I've learned a lot she said a vision
written in the sky was blown fire above the road she was
driving where the car took her   *like I wasn't even …*

two sacred storeys with some history   run down

wanted to leave but couldn't *for the glory of God* need any
shingles he said you kiddin'?

                              shingles paint bus a house even
ordination   didn't know the word   to arrange to put in order
a life she read   the cross

                          roads at Jackson and Prior
for three years in the lives of a hundred and ten drug-messed
kids   she stood   where they said

                              not just fate   two
angelic beings approached   he fed my mouth it was bitter
and out of it poured words of God   *fātum*

                                    what is spoken

on radio in the chapel on beaches on savage streets a cry
into urban wilderness   don't know what I'm saying like half
of me is standing over there when it happens   nothing to doubt
no maps no books   just the sign   *this Bible phrase has been
given to me many times*   she waits as the cards collapse
the roads rearrange

another reading

| LIQUIDITIES |

Cities, like dreams, are made of desire and fears,
even if the thread of their discourse is secret,
their rules are absurd, their perspectives deceitful,
and everything conceals something else.

ITALO CALVINO

how time exposures expose the times

wind come up in fall's green foil to Save-On Meats
opaque an hour ago lit now by sun rustle shadows one
leaf ripped off blows across bus-lit *Arbutus* floats by

        *three windows per day ... under Second
Narrows Bridge* (slack water) *can move 25 to 30
tankers per month*

Palace Hotel's lost light a strand of starling shadows
pawn shop Honest Joe's grey face gone flat   pigeon
shit stains Cosmopolitan Inn's smart pseudonym glow
red *daily weekly monthly* beyond white *walk* man's
rapid beat

        building bigger cruise *ships* bigger and
biggest   *too tall to go under the Lions Gate Bridge*

dark deepens Save-On pig's high-flying smile and cash
bag meats grow synthetic in their silver trays plucked backs
legs / 98 / 99 cent links pale under fluorescent innards paling
nuder yet

after noon's

bill put paid to young and out of our heads with ecstasy
driven re-current (over the hump that 1930s bridge) all-new drive
or lift-off from collision with what's closing in   debt paralysis now
light's red they're racketing through cost incline inclined to sail
sign for mercurial sparks of evanescent brands we're leaning into
the wind of our passing   on   acrylic legs in line in rhythm in
astro-visors unimaginable to those 1960s ones who jumped from
bridge billboard ledge fourth avenue windows looking for seventh
heaven's magnolia flesh

or sought a way out
from (through) midnight's evacuated depth sufficiently peopled
with our own reflection   tower on tower eclipse since Blackball's
splash   since Peace Parades' high

hope it's high enough for tugs at
flood tide Taylor's coach-lamp pillars raised a glow above that
human flood some 7,000 in from RR yards the wangies stickers
pokey stiffs with canned heat crack now flaring up through vein
flambeaux or stained our mirror glass is electronic tweets ten
secs at most gone digital native *If you lived under this bridge
you'd be home by now*

this city: shrouded

                      wind strum wires Jerry's Cove music standing
hulls rock in their lines virid wave on wave incoming stands of cedar
shreds through fog mimetic wind-rustle thrash or throb endless once
to hand at Jerry's camp
                  their skidders, flumes

                      their 'finest timber' towed
by the *Maggie Rogers* past Si'kheylish past Khwaykhway's standing
houses later burned

               to booms afloat to Empire booming grounds
at Gore a building boom's on track its dummy lines of ownership

slip this viridescent sheen of green onshore storm clearing the clearings
smoke shroud or fog sawdust burning off downtown as if

                       ·   this city

could re-green building transport green

                   handle a new wave now
economy size

        eco-finger its members (citizens say

antique eaten (copper) roofing o hotel hothouse hosting roof upon roof
(not by a long-handled axe though "whole paycheque" sports a vegetal
wall traffic streams down underground long wavelength desire its
disconnect

        O Jericho

        desire nets you in your strappy heels one hand
        smoothing jean skin ass-tight sashay confidence
        on the run sudden dealer stalks stock gambles
        sino forests of fraud axed at street level

faded walls of Ee'yullmough   felled long waves ago

raining buckets

                        or backward wind slant street slick
neon used to shimmer Hastings awning shelter from drip
arrays rain city housing beyond the doorway solution for
every civic fabric tearing open under (low) pressure
mouth

        making a mouth (without hands)

                                        rain-catcher

frayed collar open neck not back wet hand out

hovers hot-footing it to the curb where rain city properties
hike or dogs or tattoo (war parlour) strategies call never the
less under nimbostratus deck wind turbines turning the up
wardly (mobile) ramp to circle connective

                                a moue at this
                                coast moistly
                                mou (ill, eh?

how to weather the weather's descent on the local
farmers' bright cuisine stalls wet railyard beyond old CN
pallets of nowhere dispirited cloud of liquid drops cold
to the bone nuclei dust ice salt

                        or politicize the

pale mountains back orographic showers Salt Building's
wooden truss structure rising red from leaks abandoned
paper recycling to that cloud bank money hungers more
mouths off at wet brewpub a dank night shelter "athlete's
living room" now chronicles wet city blues cats fish rain
capital sets the mouth moves relentless eddies to current
what the city drinks eats is people

comes walking

        up through horror in the way of
vision, salt

       sh'te she'd come through walking
wood block paving cedar cracked dark wit she'll come
heron eye and quick

        kelp feather hair her stilted walk

come squawking grief transformed

through storm drain city outfall metaphor she wades
through rain's choleric traffic thrum he slows

       :that bristle shudder hers (feathers long
along her neck) and peering back intuits   disregards ...

is gone

twice shafted (*slime fisher*) diacetyl bitter bittern

       body as gift spurned   grawk

marine ah

              body of water you came wet you
come reaches of the sea through metropolis mother tide
docked and watermark culture your first growth log
saloon hotel boots you sideslip keels

                            to dwell
in habit streets you lap you shine rain's anterior head-turner
albedo gleam unfurled

                 small arm of the sea
                          fringed

infringed by dockside gantry cranes Beacon K-line rolling
stock she current *with spirit or energy a lot more than objects*
mirrors dazzle creek wise or riverine with its tip to art deco
sign Rainier's *all-woman character* once restaurant-bar its
taxi stand for 1920s black maria line-up long skirt straw
hat thought of entrance later 40s girl shoeshine smile to
his pervasive business shoe his

                       liquid lunch in the ell
bo hail below she fur b'lows in cars later incurs hardly a
culture of safety   these liquid assets about to drain

          the real

estate cult she streams through outfall tidal muck harbour
rain striated heart 'n all its submerged relations mourning
what can't be replaced   the rift   the mind   cracks in the
carefully patterned concrete

                   still Muriel mar a sign
the rain's a *place where hope comes* mildewed maybe
rusted fire escape impossible routes gnarl up through
grime to white full shine in her

               elle ll a live oh

animal sheen

              on skin's oil spotlights raise the old
Alcazar tap of heels' hurried exit then the Little boards
its must of makeup floats the York's art deco entrance
lights theatre velvet drawn live over gesture body thump
a shriek or flounce blue gel dims the thrill it's curtains
for new wave

              or New York boom (grunge Nirvana even)
alternately live and celluloid (see Palace cum Raja beauties
close up) from 1913 on (stage presence gone) til demolition
time and tense (historic) inter-
venes

echoic applause
surf traffic braking and start-ups glassy

towers loom pitfalls in memory netted as once who or
what was gutted contrail dust in collective amnesiac
flâneuring poses open stairwells

                   she was walking
her twenty something self of questionable wants
through shared streets thick with passing

fly tower and proscenium arch inchoate dark on the
blank side of the news is crow murder an act in disappearing
communitas   coyotl paws this permeable

spasm in continuity ...

whose?

a lapsed

        taste for art deco geese wing geometric read-only memory
online horizontal sunbeams (set settled) heyday that was Marine's
elevated crabs consort with streamline moderne a pattern imperial pits
and lands we read Hobb's ambition by

                              touched

with gold in morning-after fog and traffic (king i thought) he-breeze
through burnish doors and walls sequester office feet in oxford brogue
tobacco pocket clang of elevator doors that daily matinal tide on battle-
ship lino later replaced by   (bye)
                            binary data residual
tint *sea-green* slants northeast-southwest in sunny Burrard's angular
shadow labour losses hand-eye skill coordinate quick a quickening
touch by definition ice-cream melt

                        tops it   toppest (til '39) proximal
harbour beckoning world waters rising melt smelts' silver reflex glory
warped in visual stacks washed by noon anthem yaw its quick-pitch
noontide rush pedinal   pedestrian you

correct for agreement   your silver dollar shine
my dry money plant

approach

        along a log lined path sea grass trod now folk
fest crowd amped up boom adrift where herring once it's porta-
potty flattened grass or kite-snagged trees—*pick me some apples*
then   to Seal Girl's no-hand no-foot climb he shook the tree—
and down she came

        salt submerge across transformed
terrain

     refugia dream

        this rotting pier its salvaged
bridge rail salt rust and shaky (over your pole went   with the first
cast) opaque seal tears below

        here was *good camping
ground* here *spring water* long grass silt familial   unhoused

did not Jeremiah once dwell in Jericho? logger Jerry's wit lament
a different earth an iffy myth transpose

RCAF Jericho Beach air station's hangars house

seaplanes and flying boats the "Flying Seven" pilot
biplanes *woman's place is in the air* she said the base
its props and pigeon lofts await war's turn   no plot unowned

no conference unmanned   alternative Habitat Clapp view hangars'
shape of longhouse hope for community *no plastic just wood*
Reid's Haida eyes transform end wall hand-milled seating hired
an ordinary person craft dyed Rothbanners come by transit foot
or bike

     grassroots Clapp said   grass roots

        refugium

long gone   space and climate change   now anthropogenic

snowed

      blue under white diminishing habitat oblivious up
where nivean cloud feathering granite shoulder sparse col neck
infrasonic down Grouse Goat Camel Crown Fromme

                                         snowmelt
rapiding creeks drain snow line loud gravel gravelling face off
mountain down

where night news warms sky trance forms illumine towers exhale
power in the freudian body of wifi access urban unconscious
crossing a known threshold

                        mark high voltage zone

you flip your wig throw your stole over a theatre chair the show's
ongoing omnimax three-dee'd transitions the first global the *the*
they said as if permanent

                    image boxes ice where sea covered
or will where sky train and light snowdrop and sakura where war
cuts steel the intended a sprocket railway up Grouse ends

close up graupel or lattice high resolution omits touch at the
headlong rate we're going snow dulls hearing eyeblink diffusion
rhythms a different look

      Mountains' walking …

                  just like human walking.

through cloud

                        white shock blue Grouse willow ware
shades glaze those two facing Sisters hyas muckamuck
renamed couchant imperial untracked Crown looms legalized
so close down Main tonight hope snows veins eyes loose
change names liquid

                            drip eaves long gone in re-
build demolished reconstructed viz city market dream the
locals by early water under bridge no willow sole perch
sturgeon at False Creek points slaughterhouse then sawmill
muck
            mark it
                a market econ oh

who managing whose house it runs down to

                                    e-merge

a metro built on labour's back on brick or wood slats glitz
'n bling now wallow in stock collapse concrete drips snow
line no-show line down blue shopping or shipping out all
water under the bridge

                        capitalized on

Suezmax tanker traffic liquid asset runoff
liquid(i)city
                's melt oolichan near gone

it's warming up
                so grab a

rainhat eh once cedar see reigning oil's long
reach it rains for free
                    still
                        it rains

| NOTES |

VANCOUVER POEMS

Wet fur wavers: *shite* (pronounced *sh'te*), the principal performer in a classical
Japanese noh play, can be a ghost deeply attached to a certain place because
of some event or relationship that happened there in a previous life, or s/he
can be a god/spirit who inhabits that place. Here the figure of such a *shite*
joins the Western notion of a *genius loci* for the city that can, like a *shite*,
manifest in various forms.

Light, gets: Joseph Seraphim Fortes (1863–1922), actually born in Trinidad, was
Vancouver's first lifeguard, taught children to swim and saved many lives at
English Bay.

"Our city is ashes": W.H. Gallagher's eyewitness account of the 1886 fire and
Mayor MacLean's telegrams, "The Burning of Vancouver," *Vancouver Historical
Journal* 3, Archives Society of Vancouver, 1960.

"Spectacular": Alderman Hugh Bird and John R. Stead, quoted in Aileen
Campbell, "Where the Action Was ..." *Vancouver Province*, June 28, 1969, 5.
C.P. *Empress* ships described by Alan Morley, *Vancouver: From Milltown to
Metropolis* (Mitchell Press, 1961), 108–09.

For what part: my city: *Bukwis* or *Bak'was*, Kwakwaka'wakw Wild Man of the
Woods, King of Ghosts.

To navigate: *Chay-chul-wuk*, Seymour Creek, from J.S. Matthews, *Early
Vancouver: Narratives of Pioneers of Vancouver, B.C.*, vol. 2 (Brock Webber
Printing), 304.

Trails: from the ballad "Mack the Knife," Kurt Weill–Bertolt Brecht musical
drama *The Threepenny Opera*, translated by Marc Blitzstein.

Entrances: based on Franz Boas's account (with George Hunt) of the Nāq'oaqtôq version of the hāmats'a story in *The Social Organization and the Secret Societies of the Kwakiutl Indians* (Washington, DC: Smithsonian Institution, 1897), 396–400.

Terminal: *abal*, Avalon, from Old Welsh *abol*, apple.

Park, ground: E. Pauline Johnson, "The Lure in Stanley Park," *Legends of Vancouver* (Saturday Sunset Presses, 1913), speaks of "the Chinook trees." Description of the Brickmaker's Claim, Alan Morley, *Vancouver: From Milltown to Metropolis* (Mitchell Press, 1961), 21.

Old wood: Sewell Moody, temperance owner of Burrard Inlet Mills, core of the North Shore's Moodyville, the first settlement on the inlet. Alan Morley, *Vancouver: From Milltown to Metropolis* (Mitchell Press, 1961), 27.

West Coast oh: Robert M. Fripp, *Vancouver Historical Journal* 3: 79; Chuck Davis, "Year 1889" on The History of Metropolitan Vancouver website; *Kiapilanogh*, as in J.S. Matthews, *Early Vancouver: Narratives of Pioneers of Vancouver, B.C.*, vol. 2 (Brock Webber Printing), 304.

SOME OPEN DOORS

moonshine: for the Benedetti family. Peter Battistoni's memories of Union Street and Austin Phillips's memories of Hogan's Alley, *Opening Doors in Vancouver's East End: Strathcona*, ed. Daphne Marlatt and Carole Itter (Harbour Publishing, 2011).

reading it: for Annie Girard at Fountain Chapel, Jackson and Prior Streets, 1977.

LIQUIDITIES

how time exposures expose the times: Gordon Hamilton and Brian Morton, "New oil pipeline would triple capacity," *Vancouver Sun*, April 13, 2012; Brian Morton and Fiona Anderson, "Lions Gate Bridge height could curb city's cruise growth," *Vancouver Sun*, April 24, 2012.

after noon's: quote from the *Digital Natives* public art exhibition, curated by Lorna Brown and Clint Burnham, on the Squamish-owned electronic billboard at the end of the Burrard Street Bridge: a series of Tweet-length messages by and about First Nations, April 2011.

comes walking: "Smekw'a7—The Great Blue Heron," a Squamish story in *People of the Land: Legends of the Four Host First Nations* (Theytus Books, 2009).

marine ah: Doris Shadbolt wall quotation, *Lights Out! Canadian Painting from the 1960s* at the Vancouver Art Gallery, February 18 to April 29, 2012; Tom Sandborn, "'This Place Saved My Life': Inside the Rainier Hotel," *The Tyee*, August 5, 2011 (online); Sarah Ouellette's photo for March in the 2012 Hope in Shadows calendar, taken from a window of the Rainier Hotel.

animal sheen: Andrew Templeton, "The York Theatre: Saved!" *Plank Magazine*, December 21, 2008 (online); Tom Durrie, "A History of the York Theatre," August 2010 street-market handout.

a lapsed: Thad Roan, *Art Deco—Marine Building, Vancouver*, photograph, Thad Roan's Flickr photostream (online); *The Chuck Davis History of Metropolitan Vancouver* (Harbour Publishing, 2011), 164.

approach: Franz Boas, *Indian Myths and Legends from the North Pacific Coast of America*, ed. Randy Bouchard and Dorothy Kennedy (Talonbooks, 2002), 160–61; J.S. Matthews, *Early Vancouver: Narratives of Pioneers of Vancouver, B.C.*, vol. 2 (Brock Webber Printing), 300; Bruce Macdonald, *Vancouver: A Visual History* (Talonbooks, 1992), 10–11; J.S. Matthews, *Early Vancouver*, 212; Chuck Davis, "Flying Seven," on The History of Metropolitan Vancouver website; Alan Clapp, interview with Joseph Roberts, "Alan Clapp Habitat '76," *Common Ground*, June 2006 (online). "Rothbanners" refers to Evelyn Roth's contribution to Habitat.

snowed: Dōgen, "Mountains and Water Sutra," trans. Arnold Kotler and Kazuaki Tanahashi, in *Moon in a Dewdrop: Writings of Zen Master Dōgen*, ed. Kazuaki Tanahashi (Farrar, Straus, and Giroux, 1995), 97.

| PHOTO CREDITS |

DAPHNE MARLATT was at the centre of the West Coast poetry movement of the 1960s, studying at the University of British Columbia and with many of Donald Allen's New American Poets, most notably Robert Creeley and Robert Duncan. Much of Marlatt's postmodernist writing would be attuned to the adjustments, struggles, and accomplishments of immigrants. While Marlatt attended the University of British Columbia (1960–64), her literary associations with the loosely affiliated Tish group encouraged her non-conformist approach to language and etymological explorations.

She was co-founding editor of two literary magazines: *periodics* and *Tessera*, and co-editor of *West Coast Review*, *Island*, *The Capilano Review*, and *TISH*.

In 2006, Marlatt was appointed to the Order of Canada in recognition of a lifetime of distinguished service to Canadian culture. In 2009, she was awarded the Dorothy Livesay Poetry Prize, for her long poem *The Given*, and in 2012 she received the George Woodcock Lifetime Achievement Award.